This book belongs to

Useful words

(in the order they appear in this book)

astronaut

acrobat

doctor

dancer

cook

clown

bus driver

band

engine driver

explorer

postman

pirate

I want to be

HOW TO BE AN EXPLORER

Katie Carr

an astronaut.

an acrobat?

a doctor.

a dancer?

a cook.

Or shall I be...

a clown?

a bus driver.

play in a band?

an engine driver

an explorer?

a postman.

a pirate?

What do **you** want to be?

The Letterlanders

Annie Apple	Bouncy Ben	Clever Cat	Dippy Duck	Eddy Elephant	Fireman Fred	Golden Girl

Hairy Hat Man	Impy Ink	Jumping Jim	Kicking King	Lucy Lamp Lady	Munching Mike

Naughty Nick	Oscar Orange	Poor Peter	Quarrelsome Queen	Robber Red	Sammy Snake	Ticking Tess

Uppy Umbrella	Vase of Violets	Wicked Water Witch	Max and Maxine	Yellow Yo-yo Man	Zig Zag Zebra

Published by Collins Educational
An imprint of HarperCollins*Publishers* Ltd
77-85 Fulham Palace Road
London W6 8JB

The HarperCollins website address is
www.**fire**and**water**.com

© Lyn Wendon 1999

First published 1999

ISBN 0 00 303436 4

LETTERLAND® is a registered trademark of Lyn Wendon.

British Library Cataloguing in Publication Data
A catalogue record for this book is available from the British Library.

Written by Katie Carr
Illustrated by Sally Barton
Designed by Michael Sturley
Consultant: Lyn Wendon, originator of Letterland

Printed by Printing Express, Hong Kong